# queer
# baby names

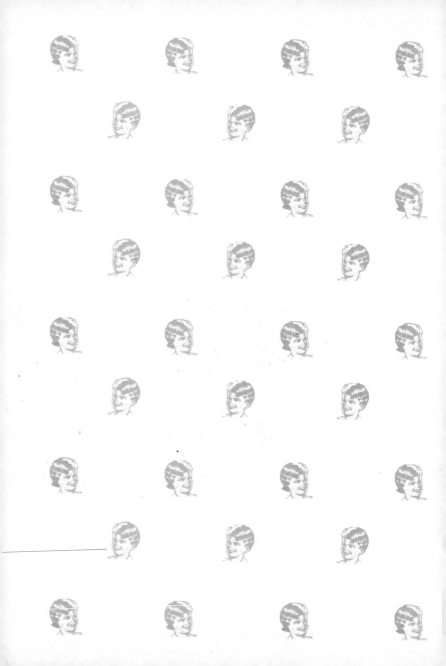

# Queer baby names

## Matthew Rettenmund & Jaye Zimet

### a completely irreverent guide to naming your lesbian/gay tot

st. martin's griffin ❧ new york

The authors would like to acknowledge Stephanie

Schwartz and José Vélez for their support,

understanding, and overall fabulousness.

Cover and interior design by Jaye Zimet

All art from the collection of Jaye Zimet

Library of Congress Cataloging-in-Publication Data

Rettenmund, Matthew.
Queer baby names / Matthew Rettenmund & Jaye Zimet.—1st ed.
p. cm.
ISBN 0-312-14711-2
1. Names, Personal—Anecdotes. 2. Gay men—Humor. 3. Lesbians—humor. I. Zimet, Jaye. II. Title.
CS2377.R49 1996
929.4—dc20    96-21481
CIP

First St. Martin's Griffin edition: October 1996
10 9 8 7 6 5 4 3 2 1

To Mack and Charlotte,
and Linda and Marv,
for starting us
on the road to queerdom.

**note:**
If you happen to have one of the names listed in this book, we are in no way suggesting that you are queer—but maybe you should be.

A name can only be a name
my name can only be my
name, I have a name. . .

—gertrude stein

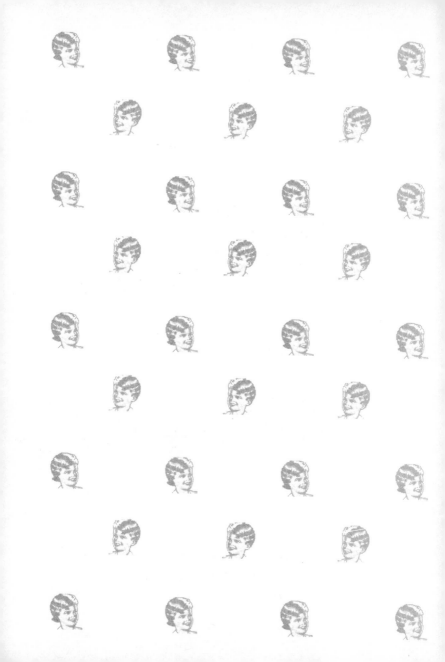

*H*ow do you plan a queer baby? You don't. ▼ You can't stack the odds by eating lots of Froot Loops or downing gallons of chardonnay, nor does it help to watch hours and hours of *AbFab* reruns—your baby is either going to be born gay or straight. ▼ But here are a couple of hints that baby might be gay...

▼ **Baby runs through pacifiers at a rate of one per week.**

▼ **Complains that blue jammies make him look fat.**

▼ **When baby is born, he arrives at least an hour late.**

▼ **Baby's first word is "Daddy."**

or lesbian...

▼ **Baby born with a perfect flattop.**

▼ **When doctor proclaims "It's a girl!" baby corrects "Young womyn."**

▼ Prefers 100% organically grown, non-animal-tested flannel diapers and baby Birkenstocks.

▼ Teethes on your back issues of *Ms.*

▼ Baby's first word is "Softball."

# the
# name game:
# an introduction
# to queer baby
# naming

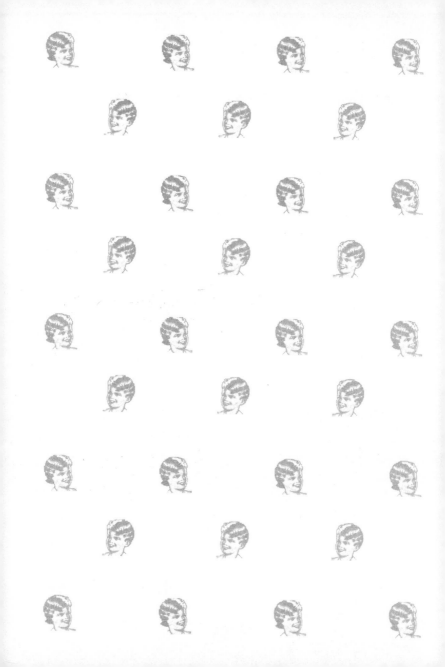

# what's in a name?

Oh, *everything.* ▼ If your queer baby is named thoughtlessly, after no one in particular and for no good reason, might not baby feel aimless? Unspecial? Suspicious that he's actually named for Mom's secret first husband? ▼ Choose your baby's name as carefully as you choose the decor of her nursery. After all, she'll outlive you. When you depart this world, there's no sense in leaving behind a baby with an ax to grind to eulogize you. ▼ You may think all baby needs is love, but get real. Image is everything. At the very least baby will need a fab collection of vintage Barbies, a Philippe Stark high chair, and a tailor-made name that screams attitude.

# the ultimate queer

## Bruce Is, Bruce Ain't

Ah, Bruce. We love you, we hate you, we *are* you. ▼ The films of Bruce Willis uphold every macho stereotype, and it'd be ridiculous to suggest that Bruce Springsteen might be AC/DC. ▼ Still, the name Bruce conjures up the image of the queerest baby alive. Only the most over-protective mom would name her son something as pre-cious as "Bruce." ▼ It helps to know that in French, the name means "from the thicket." Walk into the local park at night and yell, "Bruce?" and brace yourself for a bar-rage of replies. ▼ Bruces make the ultimate gay babies. He'll be the kid who brings his Maria Callas collection to pre-school show-and-tell. He'll wear teensy coveralls and never scuff his white baby shoes. He'll learn to do his hair before he learns his ABCs.

# baby names

## Mondo Phyllis

There are straight Phyllises, of course, but even they have a certain "queer-ness" to them that has nothing to do with their sexuality. ▼ Take Phyllis Diller, for example. ▼ Little Phyllis will go straight for the Legos and Erector sets at playtime and beat everyone to the jungle gym. ▼ Name your tot Phyllis, stand back, and watch her explore the boundaries of the social norm.*

*Author's note: We actually just picked the name because both of our junior high gym teachers' names were Phyllis....

# 6

# golden rules for naming queer babies

# right

Lesbian babies can
eliminate excess femininity in a name
by swapping it for enigmatic initials.
Forget about Jennifer Jane—it'll
morph into "J.J." before baby is
weaned. Preferred initials include
k.d. and H.D.


Boys like initials, too.
Think how popular your gay son
will be when he derives initials from
names like Brian James
or John Owen....

# #1
# androgyny
## Boy? Girl?

First, know that you can't go wrong with androgyny. Adult queer babies will appreciate delightfully ironic gender-fucking, er, gender politics reflected in their names.

**chris**—We *all* have an ex-flame named "Chris."
**jaye***
**pal**—As in *It's* _____
**terry**
**sam**

*Thanks, Mom.

# #2
## extremes
### Frilly vs. Plaid

When thinking of frilly names for boys, any traditional British boy name will have just the right amount of flounce. ▼ For girls, old-maid names lend an undeniable air of "otherness," probably because most supposedly loveless spinsters are in fact big old sex-crazed dykes.

**reginald**
**percy**
**quentin**
**alistair**
**lance**
**sebastian**

**theodora**
**hildegarde**
**hortense**
**brunhilde**
**wilhelmina**
**eunice**

# #3
# flower power
## Laying the Seeds

Flower and plant names are ideal for lesbian babies. ▼
Why is there an affinity between lesbians and flower names, you ask? It's as mysterious as the bond between lesbians and cats: deep, inexplicable, *there*.

**bush**
**pussywillow**
**blossom**
**lei**
**impatience**

The ideal name for a budding florist? Forrest.

# #4
# formal vs. informal
## To the Letter

Most formal names work for any queer-minded boy. They shudder and correct you if you call them "Benji" or "Charlie"—it's "Benjamin" or "Charles," please. It's a stone's throw away from "How dare you presume I'm straight."

Formal names that never work:

**archibald**
**ignatius**
**ebenezer**
**maximilian**

Formal names won't last long on most dyke babies. They want everything short and to the point. Like their hair.

**al** for Chantal
**izzie** for Isabella
**randi** for Miranda
**lou** for Louise
**sir** for Desirée—For that extra-attentive, eager-to-please child.

# #5
# accentuate
# the positive
## Names That Guarantee a Queer Baby

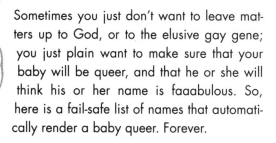

Sometimes you just don't want to leave matters up to God, or to the elusive gay gene; you just plain want to make sure that your baby will be queer, and that he or she will think his or her name is faaabulous. So, here is a fail-safe list of names that automatically render a baby queer. Forever.

The Power of Suggestion:

**gaylord**

**fagin**

**neil**—He stoops
      to conquer.

**jack**

**butch**—Yeah, right.

**guy**

**manny**

**boyd**

**frisco**

Crack That Whip—These babies will grow up making no bones about their sexual tastes. These are the kinky masters, willing servants, and fetish-mongers. Ty, Pierce, Yassir, Decker, or Scatman; Sadie, Walker (for the future foot fetishist), Mame, Obedience, or May (as in, "Mother, may I?").

If It Quacks Like a Dyke...

**amanda**—A man, duh.

**gaye**
**leslie**
**lizzy**
**butch**
**fay**
**flavia**
**reema**

## Homo-Nyms

**oral**
**peter**
**jock**
**rod**
**woody**
**willie**
**dick**
**jules**
**colin**

**juice**
**honey**
**muffy**
**pearl**
**pie**
**cloris**—Two letters away from heaven...
**cherry**
**fanny**
**palmer**

# #6
# eliminate
# the negative
## Names Any Self-Respecting Queer Baby Will Almost Certainly Have Legally Changed Later in Life

No child wants to be named after a professional asshole. ▼ Give your baby any of these "bad seed" names only if you plan to give baby up for adoption.

**rush**—Have you ever heard of child emancipation proceedings?

**leopold** or **loeb**

**newt**—Actually, *no* kid should be named after an amphibian.

**jesse**

**ronald**—For babies so charming you don't realize they're retarded until they hit high school.

**erik** or **lyle** (Menendez)

**jeffrey** (Dahmer)—Do Not Breast Feed.

**john wayne** (Gacy)

**anita**

**colorado**—She'll girlcott you.

**tammy**

**faye**

**lizzie** (Borden)

A lesbian baby doesn't want a name that brands her as (clutch the dog tags) *girly.*

> **pollyanna**—Even the name Prissy would be less prissy.
>
> **immaculata**—Unless you want baby to grow up to be a lesbian nun.
>
> **concepción**—Good *luck.*
>
> **bambi**

A gay baby boy will take offense at a name that implies he's...diminutive. Besides, it just won't work when friends are trying to fix him up on blind dates, or he's scrawling his name and number on bathroom walls.

> **junior**
> **tiny**
> **tip**
> **pee-wee**
> **les**

Instead, try **miles**.

# lucky charms: queer icons

**icon** \i - kän\ n [ L, fr. Gk *eikon* ] **1 :** a sacred image **2 :** an object of uncritical devotion **3 :** EMBLEM, SYMBOL — includes musicians, actors, sports figures, or anybody who's just famous for being famous. Icons are not born, they're made. Unless of course you're Madonna.

What Becomes an Icon Most?

A lot of "queer icons" are gay or lesbian, achieving their icon status just because they're out, loud, and proud. But quite a few are straight, and arrive at their icondom in various ways, such as:

1. By being overly camp (Judy, Liza, etc.)

2. By being fabulously flamboyant (Pee-wee)

3. Or, by being too butch for words (Jamie Lee)

# diva devotion

One of the grandest traditions of being queer is obsession. No, we're not talking about stalkers, we're talking about diva worship. Gay men do it more loudly than lesbians, but admit it, everyone has their favorite diva. *Everyone.* ▼ Screw idolatry! Why not start your baby out with a name inspired by a great gay or lesbian icon? That way, baby can aspire to know the rare thrill of being surrounded and nearly suffocated by hordes of screaming fans, as opposed to being a screaming fan who passes out and gets trampled while trying to take a blurry snapshot of some tired old superstar. ▼ And if naming a queer baby after an icon inspires baby to become an icon herself, note that the parents of icons frequently live well.

# so she wants to be a "gay icon"

**bette** (BET/ee)—"But ya *are* in a stroller,
ya *are!*"

**bette** (BET)—Baby loves baths.

**marilyn**

**madonna**—Baby cries just to see if you're
listening.

**barbra**—Giving birth to her will be like
pushing out a big stick of buttah.

**joan***

**donna**—May quietly seek to be adopted
by a straight couple.

**judy***

**liza** (with a "z")

**cher**

*If you have to ask, you might as well be straight.

# so she wants to be a "lesbian icon"

**jodie**

**greta**

**chastity**

**amanda**—Married??? With children???

**eleanor**

**marlene**

**sandra**—Without diapers, she's nothing.

**catherine**—All the girls will hunger for her.

**martina**—An icon with balls.

**katherine dawn**—Baby never grasps the concept of capital and lowercase.

# reel swish
## Hollywood Names

Don't think it's *ever* too early to take a queer baby to the cinema. Even in utero screenings will be most appreciated later in life, as gay babies need to see *All About Eve, The Women,* and *What Ever Happened to Baby Jane?* as many times as possible for accurate quoting, and lesbian babies can't get enough of that Susan Sarandon.

**rock**
**tab**
**sal**
**montgomery**
**tyrone**—Plays well with both boys and girls.
**cary**
**brad**

**drew**
**lily**
**sandy**—Glass eyes make handy marbles.
**myrna**
**capucine**
**marjorie**
**mariel**—Of all your kids,
　　　　　　she's your personal best.

# the wind beneath my wings
## Musical Names

All babies respond to music. Gay babies have a special fondness for lullabies with beaucoup BPMs, while lesbian babies tend to coo at folk songs and American classic rock. Of course, these rules are not set in stone. But one thing's for sure—show us the baby who taps her feet to "Supermodel" or "I Kissed a Girl" and we'll show you the queerest baby in the nursery.

**liberace**—Loves rhinestone diaper pins.

**elton**

**boy**

**george**

**michael**

 —the baby formerly
known as...

**melissa**

**whitney**

**olivia**

**michelle**

**doris**—Once I had a secret...?

**dolly**—A tot who'll stack up
against all the other
girls.

**phranc**

# fun and games
## Sports Names

Lesbian babies will astonish you with their sturdiness, their fearlessness with volleyballs, and their competitive natures. They'll chomp at the bit for their first putt-putt session. ▼ Boys? Eh, not so much.

**martina**
**billie jean**
~~**tonya**~~—Isn't a lesbian. She just skates like one.
**babe**
**dinah**

*Sports names are a losing bet for gay babies. In a pinch, try Greg.*

# baby

# names

# with

# character

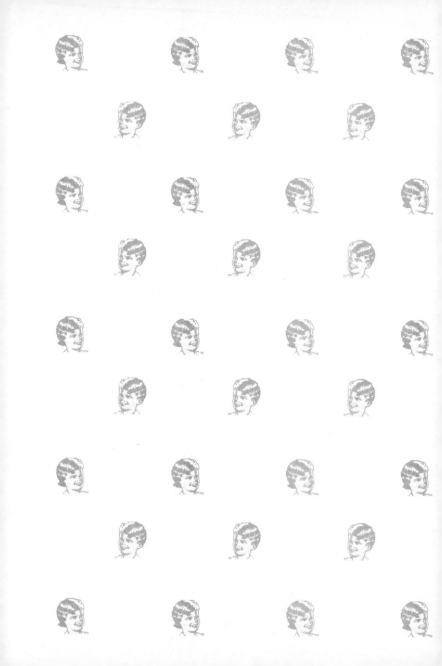

# check your local lispings
## TV Names

No queer baby alive can resist the soothing tones of PBS's goose-who-lays-the-golden-eggs, Mr. Rogers. Barney *who*? Purple dinosaurs don't cut it for these tony tots. ▼ Other TV shows enjoyed by queer babies include reruns of such shows as *Bewitched* and *I Dream of Jeannie*. Speaking of reruns, don't be shocked if your gay baby's first word is "Ginger," sputtered while watching (for the umpteenth time) that *Gilligan's Island* episode where Mary Ann hits her head and thinks she's "the mooovie star." ▼ Lesbian babies will be more interested in action-packed reruns of *Cagney and Lacey*, and they might seem particularly fond of Alice on *The Brady Bunch*. ▼ Face it—those estimates that kids watch as much as eight hours of TV a day is aiming low when it comes to queer babies.

**sidney**—*Love, Sidney*

**jody**—*Soap*

**gomer**—*Gomer Pyle, U.S.M.C.*—Well, gollly...

**mel**—*The Dick Van Dyke Show*

**darrin**—*Bewitched*

**joker**—*Batman*

**gilligan**—*Gilligan's Island*—Give up already, Ginger. And watch out, Professor.

**ellen**—*Ellen*

**darlene**—*Roseanne*

**buddy**—*Family*

**maude**—*Maude*—Right on, Maude!

**endora**—*Bewitched*

**sally**—*The Dick Van Dyke Show*

**jane**—*The Beverly Hillbillies*

# ay, caramba!
## Cartoon Names

They may be two-dimensional, whether comics or moving 'toons, but their queerness takes on all three dimensions— Queer, Cute, and Cuddly. What censor would put the kibosh on Bugs in drag, kissing Elmer Fudd? Or Marcy making goo-goo eyes at Peppermint Patty and slavishly calling her "Sir"?

**bugs**—What's *up*, Doc?
**jeff**
**akbar**
**robin**—Holy titclamps, Batman!
**linus**
**smithers**
**tin tin**—Oh, c'mon! You *knew.*

**marcy**
**patty**
**wilma**
**betty**
**velma**—More hair on *her* legs than on
Scooby-Doo's.

**lucy**
(Broome) **hilda**

# ready for their close-ups
## *Movie Names*

Naming your child from the celluloid closet might make him or her feel like a superstar. But don't be too rash—for example, you may want to screen *Psycho* before choosing "Norman."

**norman**—*Psycho*
**jeffrey**—*Jeffrey*
**molina**—*Kiss of the Spider Woman*
**harold**—*The Boys in the Band*

**varla**—*Faster Pussycat, Kill, Kill!*
**eve**—*All About Eve*
**dawn**—*Female Trouble*
**george**—*The Killing of Sister George*

# get a clue
## Queer Detectives

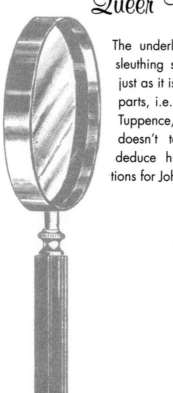

The underlying sexual tension of many sleuthing same-sex couples is palpable, just as it is for their opposite-sex counterparts, i.e., Nick and Nora, Tommy and Tuppence, Jonathan and Jennifer. ▼ It doesn't take a Sherlock Holmes to deduce his hidden homoerotic attractions for John Watson, M.D.

**sherlock** & **john**
**basil** & **nigel**
**ellery**—Major Queen.
**frank** & **joe** (Hardy)
**bosley**—Charlie's fourth angel.
**lord peter**—Is he gay or just British?

**nancy** & **george**
**cagney** & **lacey**
**jill, sabrina** & **kelly**
**jessica**—If they aren't married by 60,
            stop guessing.
**miss jane**

naming
names

# skipping to the good parts
## Literary Names

Conventional wisdom has it that some writers are indeed straight, but we know the truth: if it writes, it's queer. Marriages and hetero affairs don't prove anything. Maybe it was a phase. Or maybe jealous rivals started straight rumors.

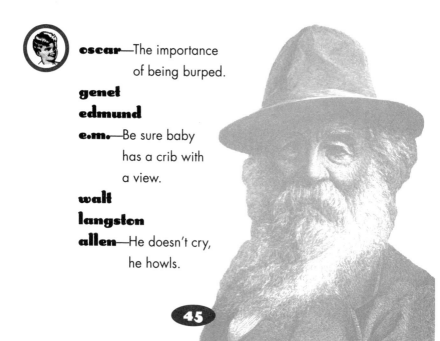

**oscar**—The importance of being burped.

**genet**

**edmund**

**e.m.**—Be sure baby has a crib with a view.

**walt**

**langston**

**allen**—He doesn't cry, he howls.

**rita mae**—*Rubyfruit Bassinet*
**emily**
**radclyffe**
**gertrude**—Dyke is a dyke is a dyke is a dyke.
**alice b.**
**anaïs**—Talk about precocious!
**adrienne**
**djuna**

# greek to me
## Classical Names

They're just following ancient history. . . .

 **narcissus**—Perhaps the first gay baby.
**adonis**
**spartacus**
**oedipus**

 **sappho**—A right-on infant.
**venus**
**electra**
**xena**—Like Hercules, except strong.

# striking poses
## *Fashionable Names*

If you clothe your queer baby off the rack, be prepared
for the consequences. Queer babies—especially boys—
want names, names, names, and we don't mean Pam-
pers. We're talking Baby Gap *at least*, but only if you're
sure Gaultier doesn't make rubber diapers.

**calvin**
**isaac**
**willi**
**halston**
**jean-paul**

*Fashion names are not tailor-made for lesbian babies. But if you insist, try Edith or Coco.*

# speech! speech!
## Political Names

Pre-Stonewall, you'd be hard-pressed to find one halfway decent queer baby name from the world of politics or the government—what were you gonna do? Call your baby J. Edgar? ▼ Naming your girl after any politically active woman will not guarantee her lesbianism, but will juice her up with a certain strength.

*For particularly active babies try Michelangelo or Urvashi*

**barney frank**—That's *Frank*, not *Fag*.
**harvey**
**dag**

*

**gloria**
**bella**
**janet**
**reno**
**hillary**
**chelsea**
**socks**—Eat your heart out, Millie.

* Haven't you heard? All feminists are lesbians. . . .

surprise!

# a queer turn of events
## Twins!

Two queer babies are better than one, and they'll always have each other to stick up for. Just make sure they don't wind up as a couple.

**bert** & **ernie**—Rubber ducky fetishists.

**bob** & **rod**—High birthweight, low IQ.

**oscar** & **felix**

**vita** & **virginia**

**edina** & **patsy**—Just hope Lacroix comes out with a line of booties.

**thelma** & **louise**

# knock-down, drag-out
## Naming Your Transvestite Baby

It may seem futile—these kids are just gonna rename themselves no matter how fab the birthname you choose, right? Don't be so sure. We all know why drag queens change names like "Bubba," but why not put baby on the right track with a knock-out stage name?

**ru paul**
**divine**
**lypsinka**
**bunny**

Use your imagination. Think of funny puns, add a vowel
or two, and you just may have a trannie baby name that
will wow 'em at Wigstock.

**mistress** _____
**bertha christ**
**hedda lettuce**
**pat o' butter**

# the last word

We're sorry if we've missed your own favorite queer name, or if the name you've selected for your queer baby has been made obsolete by our little book. ▼ But in the end, you could name a baby anything at all—it won't stunt his or her queer growth. After all, millions of us were named by clueless straight parents and look where we are today....